THE FIRST LADY WHO FOUGHT

FOR HUMAN RIGHTS

Biography of Eleanor Roosevelt
Children's Biography Books

BABY PROFESSOR
EDUCATION KIDS

Speedy Publishing LLC

40 E. Main St. #1156

Newark, DE 19711

www.speedypublishing.com

In this book, we will be learning about Eleanor Roosevelt. She was the First Lady married to President Franklin D. Roosevelt. Born in New York City, New York on October 11, 1884 and passed away in New York City, New York on November 7, 1962, she was considered an activist, a diplomat, and an American politician. Read further to learn more about her early years and life as the First Lady.

WHERE DID SHE GROW UP?

Born Anna Eleanor in New York City on October 11, 1884, she decided to be known by her middle name.

Eleanor Roosevelt in 1933

She had two younger siblings, her brother Elliott Jr., and another brother, Gracie Hall Roosevelt, who went by the name of Hall. She had a half-brother, Elliott Roosevelt Mann, who was the result of an affair her father had with a family servant, Katy Mann.

Eleanor - portrait - Huntington, Long Island, New York, 1887

Eleanor Roosevelt with her father, Elliott and her brothers, Elliott Jr. and Gracie Hall in New York

Even though she was raised in a somewhat wealthy family, she had a difficult childhood. When she was only eight years old her mother passed away, and her father then passed away two years later, when she was ten years old. These losses led her to having to deal with depression most of her life.

While her parents were alive, her mother treated her badly, and referred to her as "Granny" since she felt that Eleanor looked old-fashioned and was too serious. She was a frightened and quiet child with only a few friends that were her age. Her father was not home much, but was more encouraging to her.

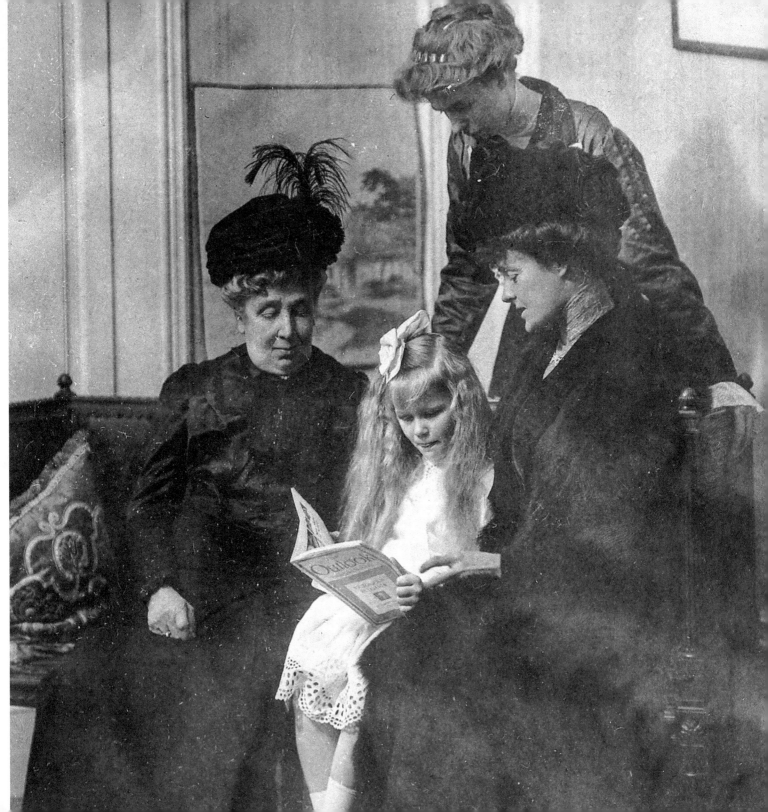

Following her parents' deaths, she went to live with Mary Livingston Ludlow, her maternal grandmother. Her childhood has been described as being starved for affection and insecure, and she thought of herself as an "ugly duckling". However, at the age of 14, she wrote that "no matter how plain a woman may be if truth and loyalty are stamped upon her face all will be attracted to her".

Eleanor Roosevelt with her Grandmother Hall,
Aunt Tissie Mortimer, and Anna in New York City

Eleanor Roosevelt at Allenswood Academy in London, England

EDUCATION

She had been privately tutored until the age of 15. When she turned 15, she was sent to Allenswood Academy, which was a private finishing school located in Wimbledon, near London, England. When she first arrived, she was fearful, but the headmistress took interest in her, and she went on to gain self-confidence along with learning to fluently speak French.

Eleanor became "everything" at the school and was loved by all. While she wanted to stay at Allenswood, her grandmother summoned her home so she could have her social debut.

MARRIAGE AND FAMILY LIFE

Once she returned to the U.S., she started dating Franklin Roosevelt, a distant cousin. He attended Harvard and was a good-looking man. They proceeded to spend quite a bit of time together and Franklin fell in love with her. They married March 17, 1905. President Theodore Roosevelt, her uncle gave her away at the wedding.

Eleanor Roosevelt in school portrait

Once they returned to the United States from their honeymoon in Europe, they decided to settle in New York City, in a house that had been provided by FDR's mother which was located in Hyde Park, and overlooked the Hudson River. She had an antagonistic relationship with her mother-in-law.

Eleanor Roosevelt with her husband Franklin D. Roosevelt

During the early years, Eleanor suffered a breakdown and as she explained it to Franklin, "I did not like to live in a house which was not in any way mine, one that I had done nothing about and which did not represent the way I wanted to live", but not much changed.

Eleanor Roosevelt with children James, Elliott and Anna in Hyde Park

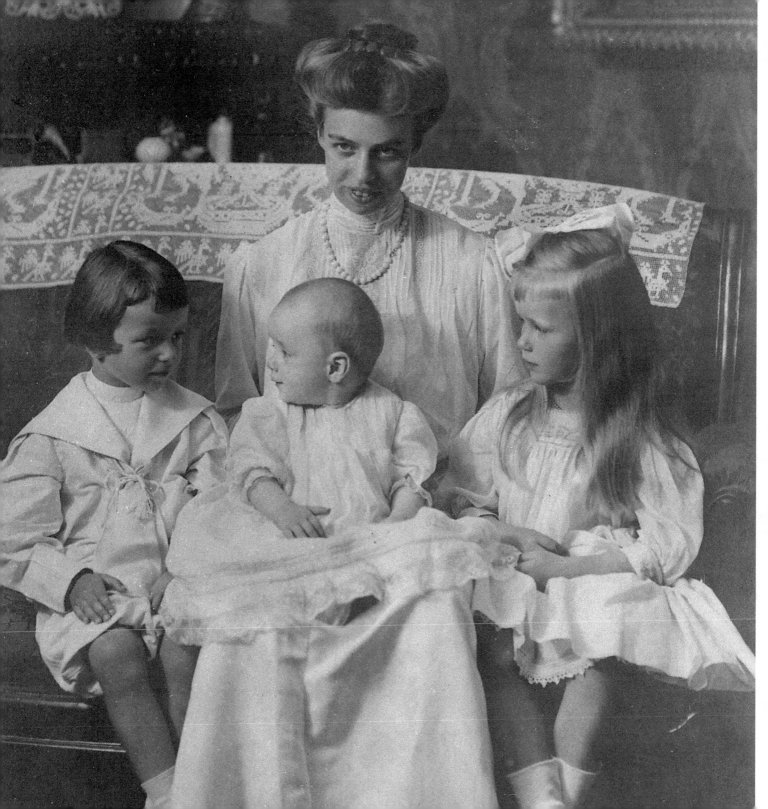

Their six children included Anna, James, Franklin (who passed at a young age), Elliott, Franklin Jr., and John. It kept her busy taking care of the children and taking care of the household.

Eleanor Roosevelt, Anna, Elliott, Franklin Jr, John, and Chief at Campobello

FDR's Illness

FDR became famous as a politician and wanted to be president. However, one summer he became ill with polio and nearly died. While he lived, he was never able to walk again.

US President Franklin Roosevelt in wheelchair due to Polio

He chose to continue in politics despite of his illness. Eleanor became determined to assist him with anything he needed. She then became involved in several organizations. She wanted to help women, children, black people and poor people to have a better life.

Detail of the Franklin Delano Roosevelt Memorial in Washington D.C.

FIRST LADY

Once FDR was inaugurated on March 4, 1933 she then became the First Lady. She was quite aware of the previous First Ladies' roles and was depressed with this new role, traditionally restricted to hostessing and domesticity. Lou Henry Hoover, who was the previous First Lady, ended her feminist activism when she took on the role.

Franklin D. Roosevelt and Eleanor Roosevelt in Savannah, Illinois

She decided it was time to redefine this position and then became known as "the most controversial First Lady in United States history". She became the first to hold press conferences and became first to talk at a national convention in 1940. She wrote a syndicated daily column for the newspaper, "My Day", and wrote for a monthly magazine column and hosted a radio show weekly, which were all firsts for the First Lady.

Eleanor and Franklin D. Roosevelt,-August 1932

Eleanor made $75,000 from her writing and lectures during FDR's first year of tenure, and gave most of these earnings to charity. She was receiving $1000 for lecture fees by 1941.

Eleanor Roosevelt with Clementine Churchill and Oveta Culp Hobby in England

She had a busy travel schedule during her twelve years as First Lady, making several appearances at labor meetings assuring Depression-era workers that the government was aware of their plight.

Eleanor Roosevelt, Adlai Stevenson and John Foster Dulles at United Nations in New York City

Planes from the USS Essex aircraft carrier dropping bombs on Hokadate, Japan, July 1945. World War 2, Pacific Ocean.

WORLD WAR II

Once the United States began moving towards war, she found that she was getting depressed again, fearful that her fight for domestic justice would again become extraneous as the nation began to focus on its foreign affairs. She considered briefly going to Europe and working for the Red Cross, however, the president's advisors dissuaded her from this idea, as they discussed the consequences if the First Lady was to become a prisoner of war.

She went on to work on other causes, starting with a movement to allow for the immigration of European refugee children and urged her husband to provide greater immigration of groups persecuted by Nazis. She was successful in securing refugee status for 83 Jewish refugees in August of 1940 from the SS Quanza, but was turned down on several other occasions.

She traveled around Europe in October of 1942, including a visit with the American troops as well as inspecting British forces. These visits drew great crowds and received mostly favorable reviews in both America and England. She visited the American troops located in the South Pacific in October of 1942 for morale-building.

Eleanor Roosevelt with an American soldier

Later, Admiral William Halsey, Jr., said "she alone accomplished more good than any other person, or any groups of civilians, who had passed through my area." She was left feeling shaken and horribly depressed seeing firsthand the carnage of the war. Several Congressional Republicans criticized Eleanor for utilizing scarce resources for this trip, which prompted the President to suggest she take a break from all of the traveling.

Eleanor Roosevelt n Galapagos Island in 1944

Eleanor Roosevelt and DeGaulle at Franklin D. Roosevelt grave in Hyde Park, New York

AFTER FDR's DEATH

On April 12, 1945 Franklin died of a stroke. Eleanor was sad, but she wanted to continue their work. For seven years, she represented the United States at the United Nations (UN), which was created in large part by her husband. While a member, she helped to write the Universal Declaration of Human Rights which described that people throughout the world should be treated fairly and had certain rights that no government should be able to take away.

After FDR's funeral, she moved from the White House, and returned to Val-Kill. Franklin had left instructions for her to turn Hyde Park over to the government to be used as a museum, so she spent the next few months arranging for the transfer. She moved to an apartment located at 29 Washington Square West which was located in Greenwich Village.

The Springwood Estate is the former home of Franklin and Eleanor Roosevelt in Hyde Park, New York. Now it is the Franklin D. Roosevelt Presidential Library and Museum.

She moved into a suite at The Park Sheraton Hotel in 1950. She remained there until 1953 and then moved to 211 East 62nd Street. In 1958, when that lease expired, she returned to The Park Sheraton and waiting for a house which she had purchased to be renovated, located at 55 East 74th Street. She had purchased this house with Edna and David Gurewitsch.

On April 12, 1946, the Franklin D. Roosevelt Presidential Library and Museum opened, which set a precedent for presidential libraries in the future.

Eleanor Roosevelt with E. Gross and P.C. Jessup at United Nations in Paris, France

Eleanor authored several books, including *This is My Story, This I Remember, On My Own,* as well as an autobiography. She went on fighting for the equal rights of women and black people. She also served for the Commission on the Status of Women as chair, for President Kennedy.

She passed away on November 7, 1962 and was buried next to FDR. Time Magazine referred to her as the "world's most admired and talked about woman".

Eleanor Roosevelt monument at the Roosevelt Memorial on January 7th, 2009 in Washington DC USA.

President Truman would later refer to her as the "First Lady of the World" in regards to her achievements with human rights.

Now that you have learned about Eleanor Roosevelt and her life as the First Lady next to her husband, Franklin D. Roosevelt, you might want to research Franklin D. Roosevelt and World War II to learn more.

CPSIA information can be obtained
at www.ICGtesting.com
Printed in the USA
LVHW062133061020
668143LV00011B/164

9 781541 910898